D1823678

Mark Quinn has always been creative. A strong desire to fulfil a childhood dream is what spurred him on to write and self-publish his first book back in 2012.

He lives in Manchester, England, with his lovely wife and furry and feathered friends.

He is active in charity work and supports a variety of local causes.

Mark's wish is to entertain and amuse people with his poems, taking them out of their normal surroundings for just a brief time while they absorb his imagination through his writing; hopefully sending them back to reality with new things to think and be curious about.

Happy reading!

This poetry book is dedicated to YOU.
Live your life,
feed your soul,
challenge yourself and others to be the best they can.
Everyone in the world is unique;
now go and show off…be proud of yourself.

Mark Quinn

LIFE AS WE KNOW IT

BY THE MANCUNIAN POET

AUSTIN MACAULEY PUBLISHERS™
LONDON · CAMBRIDGE · NEW YORK · SHARJAH

Copyright © Mark Quinn (2020)

The right of Mark Quinn to be identified as author of this work has been asserted by him in accordance with section 77 and 78 of the Copyright, Designs and Patents Act 1988.

All rights reserved. No part of this publication may be reproduced, stored in a retrieval system, or transmitted in any form or by any means, electronic, mechanical, photocopying, recording, or otherwise, without the prior permission of the publishers.

Any person who commits any unauthorised act in relation to this publication may be liable to criminal prosecution and civil claims for damages.

This is a poetry book, which is a product of the author's imagination. It reflects the author's recollections of experiences over time. Any resemblance to other works of poetry, quotes, slogans, to actual persons, living or dead, or actual events is purely coincidental.

A CIP catalogue record for this title is available from the British Library.

ISBN 9781787102736 (Paperback)
ISBN 9781787102835 (ePub e-book)

www.austinmacauley.com

First Published (2020)
Austin Macauley Publishers Ltd
25 Canada Square
Canary Wharf
London
E14 5LQ

Jeni Quinn, my wife, for believing in me and helping me compile all my poems into a single manuscript.

All at Austin Macauley, for their faith and hard work and for giving this Mancunian a chance to have his book read by so many curious readers.

Thank you all.

This is my life, this is your life, this is our life.

This book is filled with thought-provoking poems.

If you're black or white, rich or poor, male or female or 'they' or 'them'…this poetry book is for you.

Let your mind run free, not on what we CAN'T do, but what we CAN do.

From the Amazon to the melting icecaps, the forests of Borneo to the ozone layer.

Set your inner deepest thoughts on fire, get your blood pumping, get thinking – it's a beautiful thing. Enrich your imagination with what is going on in this world we all love.

What do you think about?

What is it you want to achieve?

These are evocative poems that, I hope, will blow your mind!

Culture is great and we should all be proud of where we come from…especially when we're from Manchester!

Poems

Some are crazy, some are sad,
sometimes they're funny and sometimes they're bad.
I don't write them down for any reward,
I only do it because I'm bored.
They're in my mind, I must get them out,
if I don't write them down, I'll have to shout!
So next time you see a poem from me,
let your mind wonder, let your mind free.
And keep the words inside your head…
because believe me, poetry is not dead.

The Pen

Words are more powerful with the pen.
The ink will flow, and the words will glow.
You spill your brain onto the paper,
the words pour out and have no meaning.
Your heartbeat gets stronger,
your eyes start streaming.
You look at the paper, it is gleaming.
You read it back, do you mourn?
No. A masterpiece is born.

The Metro

Waiting at the Metro station waiting for my tram;
all I could see was a woman with a pram.
An old floating crisp packet blowing in the wind;
a 'Warning: Keep Out' sign
tied with some string;
a little, dirty sparrow trying not to sing;
a dimped-out cigarette butt that should have been binned.
That's what I saw whilst waiting for a tram.
Then the woman stands up promptly, holding tight to her pram
because look no further, here comes my tram.

Suburban Town

I live in a psychedelic suburban town where lamp posts talk to each other and wrought-iron railings smile.

Where hedgehogs laugh and giggle whilst rolling down grassy hills.

Mushrooms play hopscotch on beautiful chalked markings on the floor.

Shiny black beetles paint the landscape in rich and bright colours.

Little mice ride skateboards, whilst cats and dogs make their way to work to pay for their kittens' and puppies' education.

The flowing green grass sings songs whilst dancing to the beautiful wind's chimes.

The glistening rain falls from the deep blue sky only to be caught safely by the blooming red rose petals.

This is where I live, in my mind – in a psychedelic suburban town.

Alone

In my flat all alone,
no more friends to call my own.
I sit and wonder what went wrong,
I grab a vinyl and play a song.
I wrap some gifts and watch TV,
and sit on the floor next to the settee.
I had so much a few years back,
but all that's gone I did lose track.
Will I be missed? I'll wait and see,
three years gone the end of me.

IKEA

Going to IKEA I wonder what will be,
going for a bookcase or a table just for me.

I walk in from the carpark and grab a yellow bag,
I walk around a while, then I spot a tag.

I pick a tape and pencil, and then begin to write,
I don't know what I'm doing, this is just a fright!
Maybe I'll go home, that will be alright!

Then I spot a co-worker dressed in yellow bright,
they come to my assistance and show me to the light.

I make it to the restaurant, some meatballs and a brew.
I quickly finish eating, then stop off for the loo.

I look around for arrow markings painted on the floor;
this is not so bad, I'll soon be at the door.

I spot a sign for self-serve, I'll just follow the crowd,
then I grab a flatbed trolley and have a look around.

I get my Billy bookcase, that is off my mind.
I make my way to checkouts and I'm greeted by a smile.

I haven't had service like this for a long while,
then I flash my Family Card and they tell me it's on offer!

I still have cash to spare,
so I grab a pack of Daim and throw them in the air!

Gun

It was a gun they claimed; it was a gun.
Shot in cold blood,
I did not know they were in the wood.
I did not know they were up a tree,
why, oh why, did it have to be me?

My family cried for years on end.

I picked up my bike from outside the shop,
I entered the farmhouse and heard a pop.
The door was open, so I just walked in,
I was going to pop the paper next to the bin.
I didn't know the house was being robbed,
all I was doing was doing my job.

My family cried for years on end.

I walked from the restaurant, with my wife, Honey,
he walked up to us and wanted our money.
"Take it, take it all," said Honey,
he then grabbed my wallet and all of my money.
He pulled out a gun from under his jacket,
and for no good reason he let us have it.

Our family cried for years.

Restart Your Day

I wake in the morning, I get out of bed,
I make it to the kitchen and boil an egg.
It falls to the floor and makes a mess,
I don't believe it; I've burnt my dress.
I put on my shoes and walk outside,
I close the door then close my eyes.
I don't believe it; the keys are inside,
I run for the bus and miss the ride.
My heel breaks and I fall to the side,
I gab an old lady to stop my fall
but we both end up over a wall.
I'm going to be late for work again.
Am I mad or going insane?
What a day this is going to be,
please restart this day for me.

Vegan

Being a vegan is not a fad,
I've eaten meat from being a lad.
My mother would say to me, "Stop being lazy,
chew your meat and stop being crazy.
Veggies and vegans live up trees,
there is nothing wrong from eating honey from bees.
You can't live on nuts alone,
we are meant to eat flesh and bone,
so chew your chicken and change your tone."
Then I thought, *I'm not alone!*
There's lot of people out there like me,
that want to look after the honeybee.
So, a vegan life it is for me…
and I don't mind living up a tree!

I'm Not Scared

I'm not scared to dream; I love to live.
I'm not scared of deep water; it just makes me feel uncomfortable.
I'm not scared of heights, so long as I'm safe.
I'm not scared of dogs; I just don't want to be bitten.
I'm not scared of spiders; they eat flies.
I'm not scared of snakes; they are amazing creatures.
I'm not scared of speed; it gives me a thrill.
I'm not scared of poverty; you make the most of life.
I'm not scared of anything; I'll give anything a go.

Believe

Where there is love and inspiration, you can't go wrong,
so try writing that beautiful song.
Don't give up trying to be who you want to be;
work hard at it and you will see.
Contentment doesn't come naturally;
you have to put energy in to see.
You don't get anything in this world for free.
You only need belief in one
for something to happen for you to go on,
so be that person and climb aboard
and fight for your dreams and be adored.
Believe in your ideas and be the best;
don't give up or even rest.
You can do it and beat the test
and make yourself a cosy nest.
So set up the challenge, I believe in YOU,
get out there and do what you need to do.

Starry Night

When I look into the sky at night,
I see the stars shining down so bright.
Willow the wisp and the wonky trees,
and old Ben Jones with his wonky knees.
I see an old crooked house with crooked keys,
and pebbles on the beach being washed by the seas.
The night light shines so very bright,
I even see a blind man flying a kite.
And a little child crossing the road,
looking left then looking right.
That's what I see on a very dark night,
then I say to myself, "That is not right."
This is a lovely, bright, starry night.

Tick Tock

Tick tock, tick tock.
How did it get like this?
Tick tock, tick tock.
My life feels like it's…
Tick tock, tick tock.
Standing on a house of cards.
Tick tock, tick tock.
One big gust of wind…
Tick tock, tick tock.
It will all come down…
Tick tock, tick tock.
Then it's all over.
Tick tock, tick tock, tick…

Fantastic Football

Manchester City you make it look easy,
you pass on the pitch and make it look breezy.
Your skills and techniques are a joy to the eye,
no wonder our position is so high.
We've only lost a handful of games,
but Pep has kept us on track with our aim.
Silva, 'The Magician', attacks from the wing,
Kun-Aguero shoots with a sting.
Leroy Sane's legs are like elastic,
he makes the opposite defence look tragic.
Kevin De Bruyne has an eye for a pass,
then Raheem Sterling kicks some ass!
Fernandinho and Gundogan block up midfield,
whilst Kompany and Otamendi are on the striker's heels.
A shot comes in low and hard,
but our keeper, Ederson, is still in charge.
We will win the Premier League – have no fear,
while the rest of the teams will cry some tears!

The Iron Man

Isambard Kingdom Brunel was your name,
and the SS Great Eastern was your fame.
Stuck on the rocks it did one day,
"the bigger the better," you would say.
You would work so hard and make it pay
And nobody would turn you away.
The Thames Tunnel was leaking and tragic,
but not like your children, seeing your magic.
You got a silver coin stuck one day,
but you still went to work to earn your pay;
although upside down you had to stay.
You had dreams and desires that folk would say, "Never!"
The SS Great Britain was faster than ever.
Fifteen days, that's all it took,
and everybody had to look.
Civil engineering was your game
and you put the rest of the competition to shame.
Bridges and railways all over the nation,
then your friend's Rocket pulled into the station.
Stevenson was your companion and friend,
and only two months apart was your end.
Fifty-three was no age to say,
but your ideas live on today.

Eyes Wide Open

Just do what you are afraid to do,
don't let failure stop you.
Keep on going and you will see
that you can be what you want to be.
Go confidently and follow your dream,
it's not as hard as it may seem.
You must never give up or give in,
just take the blows upon your chin.
Do not blush or be in a rush;
it will come, and do not push.
Live the life that you know can be,
and in time you will see
that deep inside you have a beautiful soul,
just be confident in your goal.
So walk that path, in-front it lies,
and look to the future and open your eyes.

Invisible

I feel the need, I have to say,
I feel my mind is running away.
I walk down the street, I'm not in view,
sometimes I go to the front of the queue.
Nobody sees the pain I'm feeling,
I feel like banging my head on the ceiling.
My illness is here for all to see,
but sometimes I feel that it's just me.
My doctor prods and then he prongs,
then he says, "There is nothing wrong."
They give me tablets and send me home,
how so much I feel alone.
Just because you cannot see,
you all out there must agree
that I need help and it isn't just me,
there are millions of others across the sea.

Humble Pie

You can face them again,
don't let them put you to shame;
remember you're on top of your game.
You made a mistake,
don't let it be fake,
for goodness sake.
Now swallow your pride,
jump back on the ride;
don't stand aside.
Show them who's who,
don't let them say 'boo';
you're a winner, not a sinner.
So, show them you're the best,
you're up to the test
and you WILL beat the rest.

To Be or Not to Be

Your time is precious,
your life is more.
Your time is now
for you to shine.
Be bold,
be better,
be a trend setter,
be a dream maker,
be a goal getter,
be a world winner.
You need to be.
To become.
To win.

The Old Wooden Door

They frantically banged on the old wooden door,
for what reason I'm not quite sure.
They kicked at it three times,
they hammered it four,
and then the policeman's foot was sore.
They had to stop for a rest,
the old wooden door was standing the test.
I wonder what was behind the door,
the bolts were holding, that's for sure.
They picked at the lock,
they searched for a key,
then they turned to look at me
because I was holding the big brass key.
They turned the lock, then dropped the key,
for standing behind was only me.

Toxic World

I open my eyes, but what do I see,
the world is full of negativity.
The inner-city's full of drugs and crime,
and people who are out from doing time.
They push a needle or smoke a joint,
they really do feel like there's no point.
The air pollution is getting thicker,
and your wallet gets taken from a street-walking picker.
The sea-life gets covered by the oil slicker,
the kids don't go to school, they just get thicker.
Our world is toxic and that's a fact
and what we all need to do is act.
So I will close my eyes and sleep tonight,
and hope in the morning I will see light.

New Day

When you awake in the morning sun,
go and start your day of fun.
Start with some exercise or just a run,
but just make sure it's lots of fun.
You have goals or dreams, of that I'm sure,
but we both know you deserve much more.
Keep on digging and then you'll reach gold,
you should never give up; you have been told.
Now write down your dreams and your bucket list,
making sure that nothing is missed.
Make yourself proud and do it for YOU,
and make others believe in you too.

Holiday Excursion

My wife said, "Let's book this, it'll be fun,"
it's eighty degrees out there in the sun.
We walked through the forest,
we've walked through the bush.
I'm not saying that we're in a rush,
but when we booked this, it was for a tour,
not to get cuts and to feel so sore.
I'm not doing this anymore.
I really do think it's just a bore.
I've walked five miles to find the shore,
and now I have no time left to explore.
My feet have blisters and are very sore,
I don't want to do this anymore.
I want a beer and to sit by the shore.
Why the hell did we book this tour?

Don't Get Too Cosy

I sit in my chair and I wonder why,
I wonder should I even try?
Try as I might, I can't get up,
my mentor said I should never give up.
So why should I bother?
I'm cosy here,
why are people shouting in my ear?
Don't give up on your dreams you fool,
don't give up on education or school.
Get off your bottom and earn a buck,
don't just wait around for lady luck.
Start to learn, get your head in a book,
start your writing or become a cook.
Don't be lazy,
don't make your life hazy.
Progression is one step at a time,
I know you can do it and you will be fine.

Don't Be Shy

Don't be shy, my little one,
you were made to shine.
You are here and here is now,
so stand up tall and let them see,
make them cheer and clap with glee,
show the world and let us see
that you can change the lives of thee.
You can make something of yourself,
your dreams and hopes you give to us.
So don't lie down, stand up and shout,
don't be a nothing or a nowt,
don't be a clown or a lout…
show the world that you do count.
Your idea is better than most,
so let us raise our glass and toast.
You will one day be that person,
for that I'm sure, for a good reason.

Our Planet 🌍

The mountains, the seas,
the valleys and the trees;
the plants in the ground
and the insects all around.
The spring showers, the summer sun,
the autumn fall and the winter sun;
the golden sands and the deep blue sea,
the feathered birds and the buzzing bee.
We take this all for granted with a pinch of the eye,
and if it all goes, we'll wonder why.
So breathe the air and take it in,
and put your plastic in the bin.
Live your life to the full,
and don't be down when it's dull.
For Planet Earth is green and blue,
and spins around just for you.

Woodland Walks

Forest mornings are the best,
they give your mind that rewarding rest.
The dew on the trees, the shining sun;
the woodland creatures having so much fun.
You breathe, you smile, you skip along;
then you hear that beautiful song.
The birds in the tree-tops hop along,
singing, singing, singing their song.
The crisp falling leaves crunch beneath your feet,
this forest walk is such a treat.
Now close your eyes and hear the sounds,
let your mind go, there are no bounds.
The cooling breeze hits you in the face,
take your time – this is not a race.
Stop and listen, what was that sound?
Was it a fox going to ground?
Was it a badger digging a hole?
Or was it just you refreshing your soul?
The sun fights hard to hit the floor;
the tree-tops cover and they do soar,
they move so gracefully up above,
did I just spot a white-tailed dove?
I hear running water from a freshwater spring,
a blue tit is calling, it is starting to sing.
This forest life is just for me,
I might just live here up a tree.
No more pollution, war or crime,
just me and creatures having a wonderful time.
This feeling I have I need to sing,
no more mobile, no more ring.

This forest adventure will be here tomorrow,
I will call again and have no sorrow.
So close your eyes, take a walk and listen carefully for that squawk,
for now you're on your woodland walk.

Universe

Parallel universe up beyond the sky,
you make me watch and you make me cry.
We swoon at the stars so bright in the night,
you are so wonderful, you're a beautiful sight.
The planets spin around from Pluto to Mars,
and we simply cannot count how many stars.
Our sun is hot and flares every day,
you're growing every second I hear people say.
A blackhole appears when a star turns to dust,
and we all stand on a molten iron crust.
The moon gives us waves and tides upon our shore,
and we will explore you just a little bit more.
Matter, dust, clouds and light,
you are such a tremendous sight.
So here is to a billion years more,
and to your growth, I know you will soar.

Succeed

How you look is how you feel,
keep your faith, push fear away.
Treat others how you'd liked to be.
Stand up tall and breathe in deep.
Do your thing, don't be a sheep.
The world is your oyster, you are the pearl,
you make the world spin; you make it swirl.
So never give up on what you believe,
you know you can, you can achieve.
Keep your dreams alive, at least give it a go,
don't give up now, put on a show.
Challenge yourself and you will grow
and in the end, you will glow.
So start that business or venture be,
and in the end you will see.
If you work hard and keep to your plan.
You will achieve, you will succeed.

Rainbow Child

The rainbow child is shy and silly,
she lives in a candy house with Milly and Billy.
She has candy floss for cushions and unicorns for friends,
and there's loads of gold where the rainbow ends!
She runs and hops over coconut stones,
and for her dinner she munches on red jam on scones.
Her hair is the colour of red, white and blue,
and the chickens bark, and the donkeys moo!
She plays and runs for endless miles,
and at the end she's still all smiles.
The rainbow child is full of joy,
she laughs and giggles with her favourite toy.
So next time you see a rainbow above,
smile and wink and give it some love
because the rainbow child is watching you
and sending back hugs and kisses too.

Chin Up

As I sit down in my chair,
I wonder why
I stare and glare.
Did I fail or just unrail?
Failure is just a setback,
I will get back on track.
This is not defeat,
I'll soon be on my feet.
Moving on is what I do,
my inner strength will shine through.
This is a blessing in disguise,
I will stand up tall,
I will survive.
This will not get me down,
I will not frown.
I have faith in me,
for the person to be.

Mind Blind

I don't know what's happening to me,
I don't know what life is supposed to be.
I don't know what will become of me,
my mind is blind, I cannot see.
I need to get a grip,
be the person I want to be.
I will not run, nor will I hide,
I will not push my friends aside.
I think of the past, the years move fast.
I have to act now, but I don't know how.
Should I give up?
NO. I need to buck up!
I need my negative mind to shut up!
I'll turn this around, everything will be sound.
I have my family around, I will not go to ground.
I shall dig deep and get out of this heap,
life will be kind and will clear my blind mind.

Drip

I walk in, out from the rain;
drip, drip, drip, dripping.
I kick off my shoes and hang my coat;
drip, drip, drip, dripping.
The rain pours down, the gutter is broke;
drip, drip, drip, dripping.
The cat-flap flaps and in runs the cat;
drip, drip, drip, dripping.
I look out the window to see the umbrellas bobbing;
drip, drip, drip, dripping.
The lightning flickers, the thunder cracks;
drip, drip, drip, dripping.
The clouds shift and the wind howls;
drip, drip, drip, dripping.
The heating now on and cuppa in hand;
sip, sip, sip, sipping.

Predictions

The seas are vicious, do you agree?
There will be no land for you and me.
The rocks do crumble, the hills do slide,
the wildlife creatures, they need to hide.
The world will end hundred years from now,
I wish we could stop it, but don't know how.
The oil runs dry, the gas will stop,
and all the volcanoes will go pop.
Our health will fade, we will need shade,
the sun is that hot and the corpses rot.
The trees are all gone there's no oxygen,
we're all dying quick and I feel so sick;
I wish this was all a horrible trick.
This does suck, I wish you all luck,
and this is all because we didn't give a f@#k.

Oasis in the Sun

Oasis in the sun, you stole my heart,
your whitewashed houses are an art.
The pebbled beaches, the deep blue sea,
you really mean the world to me.
The rooftop tavernas and bars below.
The many gift shops that line the streets –
it really is a fantastic treat.
The donkey trips to the Acropolis;
there are no lager louts on the piss.
We stroll the cobbles in the day,
there are so many shops I have to say.
Some of the finest food and sights to see,
I will return with so much glee.

Chair-Gazing

I sit in my chair and I gaze into space,
I think of all the human race;
I wonder what they are doing now,
I stand from my chair and take a bow.
How important are they to me?
Just as important as the land and the sea;
I need you and you need me,
we'll plant the seed and grow the tree.
We will dream together and live in peace,
there are no bounds in our mental state
and no room on our Earth for hate.
We can live together and share our love,
don't look down but stare above.
We only need a few to spread the word,
so let's stand out from the herd.
Let's put our dreams to the test,
do not stop and do not rest,
and if anything, do our best.

Light at the End of the Tunnel

Everyday gets a little bit better,
everything seems to be a little brighter,
the weight on my shoulders is getting lighter.
I can see light at the end of the tunnel.

My mood is getting sharper,
my nerves are getting stronger,
my breathing is getting clearer.
I can see light at the end of the tunnel.

My joints are getting smoother,
my mind is not so foggy,
my tears are starting to dry.
I can see light at the end of the tunnel.

My worries are starting to fade,
my bitterness is in the shade,
my friends come to my aid.
I can see light at the end of the tunnel.

The light shines bright,
I know I'll be all right.
I have found the light
at the end of the tunnel.

Broken

If you feel broken or down in the dumps,
don't despair
raise your arms in the air;
say these words so everyone can hear…
"If I am broken, I can be fixed,
I don't need a box of fancy tricks.
I don't need a wand or a magic stick.
I will not stay broken,
I will be fixed."
Now wiggle your fingers and wiggle your nose,
touch your feet and tickle your toes.
Do you feel better?
I bet you do.
You are not broken,
you're just you!

Mind Vision

I awake in the morning, I can't see the trees,
I can't even smell the honey or hear the bees.
My mind's eye vision is blocked by the dark,
I feel like I'm treading water and being followed by a shark.
Why can't I just be like the surfer dude?
I'm not complaining or being rude.
I just need vision on where I need to be,
but nobody understands and they cannot see.
I feel like my mind is going to explode,
nobody can help me, I will not be told.

Wisps

There is more out there, you will see.
There is more out there when we die.
There are more out there, we'll be up high.
Wisps in the dark, we will be.
Wisps in the dark, we will be free.
Wisps in the dark, we will see
other wisps in the dark full of glee.
They wisp about the moonlit sky.
They wisp about so very high.
They wisp about, I do not lie.
In and out of space they go.
Maybe four or five in a row.
So next time you feel all alone,
do not moan and do not groan.
For look to the sky and you might see,
a little bright wisp smiling down on thee.

Three Shovels and a Bucket

The year 1665 was hell for London town.
It was very hot the August heat,
the bells rang many times over the muck-covered street.
There was death and pain everywhere.
More cats and dogs had to die,
but that left rats to run and be sly.
The fleas fed on the blood of the weak.
Red cross on the door and a chain locked you in.
Why would that be? You've committed no sin.
Blood from your nose, being sick in a bin.
Locked in your home to die in pain.
Death pits dug whilst the town folk shrug.
The grave-digger digs whilst his father dies.
Cysts under your arms or on the groin.
I search daily then I find,
my time has come for me to die.
The frost falls thick from way up high,
it ends the plague; we say goodbye.
I was the grave-digger and my tools are now sold,
my poor old mother must bow and fold.
Offered four shillings for the tools of the trade;
three shovels and a bucket,
that's all she made.

World Attacked

The sky burns orange with glimmers of red,
I can feel this strange feeling pounding my head.
The climate seems sticky and hard to breathe,
I look at the people, they're ready to leave.
Then the rocks of fire come falling from the sky,
the clouds roll back and vanish so high.
We run for our lives whilst ducking and diving,
will anyone be left? It's a fight for surviving.
The clothes are burning while still on people's backs,
I think the Earth is under attack.
I hide under a tree to shelter the hail,
one hits the tree and then splinters, I bail.
Laser rays appear from afar,
the roads are now just molten tar.
It's hard to run, then I look towards the sun.
I can't believe my eyes, I can't believe the size.
Is that a spaceship?
Then I trip
and fall to my knees,
oh my God, no…please….

Lost

Jungle life is every day,
jungle life we live and play,
jungle life I want to stay,
jungle life I hope and pray.
The jungle trip was great until
our guide, he took us for a ride,
he left us to one side,
he took off with all our cash
and treated us like garbage trash.
Now that we are all alone,
just me, the wife and Mrs Slone,
we must make it on our own.

The river flows rough down the valley below,
we must carry on walking, we're going too slow.
Can we build a raft? Or are we being daft?
Make it from timber, our sailing craft.
The rapids are dangerous, the raft breaks up,
it hits a rock and we come unstuck,
the craft is no more so we swim for shore.

We must walk from here, but I sense great fear.
The leopards hide and wait for dark,
the red ants cover the towering tree's bark.
I hear the cry of a jungle lark.
The blowfly burrows under your skin,
my canister of water is running thin.
Will this nightmare ever end?
This jungle is driving me around the bend.
Can I text? My phone won't send.

Mrs Slone, she lost her hat,
down from the trees came a bat
and took off with her floral hat,
then she tripped on a large rat.
"T#@t!" – I never heard her swear like that!

The night draws near,
and so does the fear.
Mrs Slone, you are dear,
out from her handbag three bottles of beer.
I go for a pee behind a tree,
I cannot believe it, I'm full of glee,
you wouldn't believe what I can see…
a coach-load of tourists staring back at me!

Jennifer, Guinevere, Gwenhwyfar

Jennifer, Guinevere, Gwenhwyfar.
You are the woman of my dreams,
you are the captain on my team,
you pull on my heart strings and make it beam,
when my coffee is black, you are my cream.

Oh Jennifer, Guinevere, Gwenhwyfar.
You have a heart of gold,
when we first met, you had me sold,
your body keeps me warm when the weather is cold,
you are so beautiful, you have to be told.

Oh Jennifer, Guinevere, Gwenhwyfar.
You make my mind swirl,
you make my knees twirl,
and if I had hair, you would make it curl,
but most of all, in my oyster, you are my pearl.

Pets

They bark, they purr, they run around,
they growl, meow and talk their sound.
You take them for a walk, they run around,
chase a mouse,
then make a mess around the house.
Their claws are sharp,
their teeth do bite,
balls of fur, oh what a delight!
Your curtains get pulled,
your slippers get chewed,
oh my dear, they've gone and pooed!
You feed them wet,
you feed them dry,
they pull your trousers,
they claw your thigh.
You watch TV,
they sit on your knee,
you cannot move,
you cannot see,
then oh my dear, they have a pee!
What would you do without your friend?
You will walk and feed them till the end,
and all because…they're your furry friend.

Deadly Sea

The trawler's bobbin' out in the sea,
the cabin boy waits to make the tea;
it's dark and unforgiving, the deep North Sea.

The trawl is set,
overboard goes the net,
the trawlermen play cards for a penny a bet.

The otter boards open the net like a kite,
it's a long hard trawl throughout the night.

The skipper sets the course,
the trawler heads west,
he's been at it for years,
he knows best.
The men have worked hard, they need their rest.

The winch starts pulling the net from the deep,
the first mate is shattered, he needs his sleep.
The cod end is opened,
the catch starts to pour;
crabs and herring all hit the floor.

Then a bang in the boiler room,
black smoke bellows out.
"Make for the small boat," the skipper does shout.
Nine men in a dingy watch in shock,
the trawler is sinking
and they're miles from dock.
The rain starts pouring,

the boat fills up,
the waves get bigger,
the men start to shiver.

Then without warning, the boat starts to sink,
the men now know that death is on the brink.
What can they do?
They don't know what to think…
then one by one they begin to sink.

The North Sea is dark,
it's a grave to some of the best,
but at least now the nine will be at rest.

The Surfer Dude

He lives his life for the waves,
he lives his life to sunbathe;
he lives his life to have no hate,
he lives his life to fish with bait.
He lives his life with no stress,
he lives his life how he wants to dress;
he lives his life in his bubble,
he lives his life with no trouble.
He lives his life with no fear,
he lives his life full of cheer;
he lives his life to the full,
he lives his life, it's never dull.
The surfer dude is relaxed and calm
and resting under a shady palm.
So next time somebody is being rude,
remember, you're a surfer dude.

The Funky Jungle

If elephants wore lipstick,
what would it be like?
If the seahorse laughed at the lion's joke,
and the snakes and spiders all drank coke?
If the monkeys danced whilst playing the flute
and then told the poodle, "You'll never be vicious you're just
too cute!"
Then the ants started tap dancing, that was a sight,
the crocodile wore heels and then started a fight!
The hyena started laughing whilst flying his kite,
while the lady giraffe looked sexy in black nylon tights.
The parrot stopped flying because he was scared of heights...
and all because the elephant wore lipstick on a Friday night!

The Positive Man

The positive man stands tall,
he will not fall,
he takes the right steps and makes the right moves;
yes, that is the positive man.

The negative man is yesterday's man,
not in the mood,
doesn't want to move;
yes, that is the negative man.

The positive man gets the early worm,
makes the right choice
and scores his goal, then cheers with delight.

The negative man walks in a slump,
looks down to the floor and cannot score,
he hits the post, then falls to his knees.

The positive man can see ahead,
he has a plan in his head.
He writes his goals down in his pad
and yes, he can be sad,
but the positive man loves to live
and will give all to make his mark.

The negative sees no path ahead
and his goals are rattling about in his head,
and when he is sad, he makes it worse
and can see no point in the universe.

I Did the Garden

Today I did the gardening a different way;
I used a knife and fork to cut down the trees
and a wooden spoon to support my knees.
I cleaned out the hive for the bumblebees.
I pulled out the weeds with a set of pearl beads.
Then, whilst on my head, I planted more seeds.
I trimmed down the hedge with next door's dog,
then brushed up the leaves with an old wooden log.
I turned over the soil with a roll of tin foil,
then switched on the kettle and watched it boil.
I had a nice cup of tea whilst sat up a tree.
I told you I did the gardening a different way,
I told you so,
I told you today.

Sdrawkcab No Seohs

If I put my shoes on backwards
what would the world be?
Would the world spin opposite to you and me?
If I turned on the switch,
would the light go off?
If I blew my nose,
would it give me a cough?
If I turned on the cold tap,
would hot water flow?
If I dampened somebody's spirit,
would they then glow?
If I turned off the gas and lit a match,
would it blow?
If I broke my car,
would it then go?
This could happen, it's all 'ifs' and 'buts',
so I'll keep my shoes on the right way,
thank you very much!

Pendle Witch

Lancaster Castle many years ago,
the court rooms did put on a show.
Up Pendle Hill it was such a hike
to find the tower of Demdike.
Was she a witch?
We'll never know.
Could she do magic?
Or was it a show?
August 16th, 1612 was the day in court,
throwing her life away and held
in the Well Tower for months on end,
sending poor Demdike around the bend.
Her grand-daughter, only nine
had her time to shine.
Jumping on the witness stand
and sending ten off to hang.
Pointing the finger at all her clan,
was the court just an almighty sham?
It did not matter that fateful day
for in the end, 12 did pay.

My Writing Room

Writing room,
yeah writing room,
you give me so much zoom.
You cancel all my gloom
and it all comes from within this room.
My inspiration comes from within your walls,
like the leaves when autumn falls.
You make my blood run cold
when a story of murder unfolds.
I look out your window at the night sky,
then I hit a high with a story about a guy.
There's nothing special about this guy,
until I finish his profile –
then he's a spy.
Then when I get writer's block,
your vibes give me such a shock
that I start to think of Mister Spock!
And then I write a space story that will shock.
The pictures on your dark blue walls
help me think, then a character calls.
The ink in my pen starts to run,
as I write about a dangerous nun.
You are so ace,
you truly are my special place.
If my next book is a boom…
it's down to you, my writing room.

You, Only You...

Don't blame your parents for the way you act;
they gave you a body, now that's a fact.
Your mind is your own of endless powers.
You've been in the making for as long as time,
and if not yet, your time will shine.
Be yourself and don't be hard;
you are what you are, you have come far.
So shoulders straight and head up high,
don't be negative, say goodbye.
Positive motivation is what you need;
what you become is what you feed.
Live your life with no regrets,
no hard feeling or heated threats.
Let your soul be free
and be happy, with loads of glee.

If

If I was a bird, I would fly so high,
I would fly that high I would hit the sky;
I could pass people by
because I would be that high.
If only I could fly…

If I was a mole, I would live in a hole.
Underneath the busy street,
I would munch on many a tasty treat
and be way under the marching of feet.

If I was a monkey, I would live in the trees
and swing along with such ease.
I would eat the fruits that fall from above
and give the trees all my love.

If I was a snake, I would slither along
whilst singing about a happy song.
My heart would be full of glee
and very grateful for all I could see.

I am a man who feels all above,
in my heart is so much love.
I can be what I want to be
and in my soul I feel so free.

Our Cats

We have cats,
five at that,
they live in our house
with a toy mouse.
They keep us going,
they keep us alive,
that is why
we have five.

Bramley Apples is our first,
she can run with a burst.
She's all black and can attack;
three single strands of white hair
and her green eyes have a hypnotic stare.

Next in line is our little swine,
Branston Pickles is his name,
he keeps all the girls on their game.
Tabby and white is his fur
and he has a lovely purr.

Then comes our Ginger Nut,
her bell-bell is the best;
full of fur, it beats the rest.
She sleeps in the bathroom within the towels,
then when it's dark, she's on the prowl.

Then the twins, Thelma and Louise,
and believe me they are a tease!
Thelma is a tabby and white,
she always jumps out and gives me a fright.
Louise is a black and white,
she can scratch and she can bite,
but only in play I must add,
and she never makes us sad.

Our furry family give us joy –
four girls and a boy.

The Man That Walked
a Million Miles

The man that walks a million miles
has on his face a thousand smiles.
His body burns from head to toe,
his muscles burn and his tendons glow.
The man that walks a million miles,
his life is full of turmoil and trials,
that's the man that walks a million miles,
but he keeps a thousand smiles.
His life is hard, but he doesn't moan,
because in his mind he sits on a throne.
That is the man that walks a million miles.
He never gives in,
he never moans aloud;
his voice is so calm.
He will never shout;
that is the man that walks a million miles.

Paris for My Birthday

Saturday afternoon in Paris,
rushing for our plane.
We hit the sights one by one
whilst hopping on the train.
The sun is shining hot in the sky,
there's not a spot of rain.
I hope we make it to the airport
for our two o'clock plane.

Time goes so quickly,
we're at the airport and feel so sickly.
We catch our flight just in time.
And now for a rhyme within a rhyme...
"Oh, Air France you are the best,
complimentary drinks and the rest.
You fly so high, you beat the rest.
We enjoyed the flight you are the best."

We arrive in Manchester in just over an hour.
We go through customs with speed, such power.
We jump in a cab, this trip has been FAB.
Thirty-three hours we have been away,
but now we're back home and here to stay.
Our trip to Paris was one to remember.
It was for my 50th, the 14th of September.

We saw the Tower, the windmill and more,
now my wife's feet are so very sore.
At the end of the day, the trip was a thrill,
Paris, the city, you are just brill!
We will be back to enjoy the Seine,
even in the pouring rain!

DPRK

If wolves battered down your door
then knocked you to the floor,
leaving your nation battered and sore –
would you now lock your door?

Don't let anyone in,
protect your homeland with a gun;
well that's what happened with Kim Jong-un.
We should let them be,
let them be free,
maybe one day we will see;
there will be no bang,
just a party in Pyongyang.

They may have their problems, and so do we,
we're not always happy with joy and glee,
so let's go to the demilitarized zone and plant a tree.
We can watch together as the tree grows tall
and see all the nuclear weapons fall.

The Korean Peninsula will one day be one,
there will be no tears and be no bomb.
So, let's open our arms and hold out our hand
and shake on a deal, that will be for real.
Keep our world safe and drop the gun…
Come on, Kim Jong-un.

Halloween

I got told this story a few years ago,
the man in question should be on death row.
Multiple killings and blood everywhere,
people would look, and people would stare.
The slaughter would flow, and his axe would blow,
blood would pour down the gutters below.
A dozen bodies they found that week,
who IS this terrible, monstrous freak?
He will kill women and he will kill men,
he did kill nine, no wait, it was ten.
It comes about every two to three years,
his victims look on in floods of tears.
Look out of your window, the time is near,
and believe me this, you should fear.
He will come for you, no questions asked,
you could be at the sharp end of his axe…

Footprints in the Sand

You walk on the golden sand,
you leave your footprints behind.
Loving memories burn in your mind,
your natural beauty shines on your face;
you are so kind.
You're top of the human race.

This is the structure of what you've become;
the way you live, the way you give,
your spirit, and the way you love.
You're a blessing in sweet disguise,
you really are a prize.

You should be proud of what you've become,
you challenge yourself,
you live your dreams,
you conquer your fears with very little tears.
You are the sun, the rain and the winter's snow,
and on a dark night you just glow.

So stay as you are, that shining star,
and I just know, you will go far.

Thank You

That was for you, that was for me,
it was also for the man up the tree.
It was for the woman in the hole
and the striker who scores a goal.
It was meant for him who is about to sin,
and the lonely tramp looking in a bin.
It was meant for a child, a dog and a cat,
and even the little dirty rat.
So you can see it was meant for all,
so stand your ground and stand up tall.
Do not fight and do not brawl,
do not get on your hands and knees, and crawl.
It was for the soldiers who fought for us,
it was for the heroes who died for us.
It was for you all, wherever you are,
it was for the people near and far.
So again, I thank you for being you
and for playing your part on this Earth too.

The Cooking Kitten

If a cat could bake,
what would it make?
Would it make a carrot cake?
By using a garden rake?
Oh my, for goodness sake!
If a dog could fish,
would it use its dish
to catch the fish?
Or a snake? And would it hiss?
If a monkey could sing,
would it rap and wear bling?
Would the primate sing on stage?
Would it cause a rage?
If a goat could sail a boat,
would it keep it afloat?
Would it sail the seven seas
and go wherever it pleased?
Make your life strange and fun,
do not hide and do not run.
Stand up and be heard.
Be proud and stand out from the herd.

Santa and You

The snow is falling outside the door
whilst the hot chocolate melts, then it will pour.
The tree is glistening colours of red and green,
and the gifts are wrapped so as not to be seen.
The candles are lit and looking so fine,
you look at the clock and notice the time.
You should be in bed and cuddled up to big ted,
because very soon the man in red
will be putting more gifts at the end of your bed.
So don't be naughty – no matter your age.
Never get angry or show any rage.
Be a good elf and get off to sleep,
Santa doesn't want you to sneak a peek.
Sleep tight and all your dreams will come true,
and believe in Santa – because he believes in YOU.

Rainbow

If I were a rainbow, what colour would I be?
Would I be blue like the sea?
Would I be green like a tree?
If I were a rainbow, would I have gold at the end?
Would I drive you around the bend?
You bet I would!
If I were a rainbow, I would brighten up the sky, I would be
that high.
If I were a rainbow, I would have colours of yellow, pink and
green;
I would be a mean machine.
If I were a rainbow, I would have leprechauns guarding my
treasure
and two unicorns – just for good measure.
If I were a rainbow, I would need the sun and rain to shine,
But I know in the end that you would be mine.

Christmas Tree

Christmas time is here again, and you'll have such a ball,
the Christmas tree stands tall and proud in the living room, or
the hall.
The Christmas tree lights shine so bright,
you have to close your eyes real tight.
The tinsel hangs and the baubles dangle,
the candy canes are at an angle.
Your Christmas stocking hangs over the fireplace swinging
back and to.
You've just been playing snowball fights, your fingers, oh so
blue!
You enter the warmth of your home for hot chocolate and
gingerbread,
just before a flying snowball hits you in the head.
Time is getting on, you must get ready for bed,
time to rest your tired feet and your weary head.
Santa Claus will be with you soon, placing gifts under your
tree,
and when you wake in the morning, you'll be full of glee!
So have a happy holiday this year and have a drink with me,
and please remember to have fun and decorate your Christmas
tree.

The Man on the Stairs

The man on the stairs just sits and glares,
He has no worries, he has no cares.
The man on the stairs is a rich man by far,
he has no money – that's for sure –
and his problems are just a blur.
The man on the stairs loves to love,
loves to care
and loves to share.
The man on the stairs has memories
of joy and happiness that lasts,
and he makes sure his life is a blast.
The man on the stairs just sits and glares,
he has no worries he has no cares.

Moles

There are three moles who live in three holes,
and each and every one of them have golden souls.
They dig their holes all day long
and disturb the gentlemen playing crown green bowls,
then pick up loose coins on the motorway tolls!
They all play with porcelain dolls
and go to battle with devilish trolls.
But most of all, they have big fat hairy goals.

Hazy Days

Lazy hazy days with lazy hazy hair
sat in a big comfy chair.
Lazy hazy Kay and crazy lazy Ray drinking soda
off a crazy-coloured tray.
This is the life, no trouble or strife,
having a lazy, crazy, hazy day with Kay and Ray.

I

I live to love and love to live,
I love to talk and love to walk,
I love to think, I love to blink,
I love to share, and I love to care,
I love to hear, and I love to see,
but most of all, I love to be me.

Imperfections

Imperfections in us all,
there are imperfections in a wall;
imperfections we must not call.
Sometimes things can go wrong,
like writing a play or singing a song.
You may think it's just you,
you may not have a clue.
Imperfections are not all that bad,
imperfections should make you glad;
your imperfections are what you are,
and believe me, you're a blinking star.

The Past

The past is the past.
Yesterday has gone,
but today you can be at one.
Yesterday might have been bad,
but today you should be glad
you can breathe in the air and not give a care.

The past is the past.
Yesterday will never be back,
you should stay on track.
Look to the future, my friend,
and don't go around the bend.

The past is the past.
You can never bring it back,
you should look to the stars and move on fast
because the past is the past.

Temporary Insanity
A True Story

Seeing mermaids on the chair,
seeing aliens in the air,
seeing my home changing shape,
hearing voices, acting ape.
Telling lies with googly eyes
and nearly saying my bye-byes.
Seeing a black boy in my room,
spraying water bottles,
aliens go BOOM!
4 AM and walking in the park,
wearing summer clothes in the dark,
locking my father in the yard,
the local pub telling me I'm barred!
Four Non-Blondes playing on my deck,
my Uncle Billy is such a wreck,
hearing voices but nobody's there,
my family did worry, they did care.
My temporary insanity lasted two whole days
and after that it wasn't a haze.
I'm glad I did become sane
because I nearly jumped through the windowpane.

I Can

I can see,
I can hear,
I can feel,
I can fear,
I have belief,
I feel grief,
I can love,
I can hate,
I can touch.
I can feel because this world is real,
so go out there with the right attitude
and feel the gratitude.

Do?

That's what I do,
that's what you do,
this is what they do,
this is what we'll do.

Do I do what I do for fun?
Do you do what you do,
or do you run?
Do they do it because they do?
Or do we do it because we haven't got a clue?

So, what do we do?

Reality

Reality to me might not be what it is to you;
I see green, do you see blue?
I see the sand, do you sea it too?

Reality is in the eye,
I see land, you see sky.
I see a cat, you see a dog,
do I see a twig and you see a log?

Really, do we all see the same thing?
Is everything black and blue?
Do I see me, and you see you?
It doesn't really matter what we see,
as long as our hearts are full of glee.

Grow Up?

Why should we grow up?
Why can't a dog always be a pup?
Our life is too short to be sad,
we should make the most of it and be glad.
Time stood still when you were a kid,
but soon they could be nailing down the lid!
Get off your arse and make love,
free your soul, be like a dove.
Grow old if you must,
but don't be decrepit and rust.
Wake up with a smile on your face
and smile at the human race.

Prat

When someone's a prat, let it be that,
just laugh and smile inside,
don't let it spoil your pride.
Don't let it upset your day,
karma will pay
and don't let it dampen your day.
Your life's balloons are yours to keep,
don't let anyone have a peep,
because some people will try to make your day worse –
and those balloons should not burst.
Your happiness is important to you,
and the rest know what they can do…

The Magical Garden

The magical garden is such a find
and there is only one of a kind.
The trees are green, and the fruit must be seen;
pink and purple tangerine.
They hang from the branches in bunches of six,
then fall to the ground in a colourful mix.

The flowers are bright like a shining star
and can be seen, long and far.
The grass is so lush and the bramble bush;
so, relax and do not rush,
for the magical garden is in your head
and you can dream about it whilst in bed.

So have sweet dreams and don't be snappy,
for the magical garden will make you happy.

Dream

Do chickens dream?
Do budgies scream?
Do cats like art?
And do dogs fart?!
Do rabbits snore?
Do eagles soar?
Do lions roar?
And do fish like apple core?
Do apes take a bath?
Do giraffes laugh?
Are most of the world's zebras called Kath?
Our animal friends are becoming rare
and this world can be so unfair.
So, let's be kind and let us care.
Spread the word and let us share.

Don't Let Them In!

The environment you're in should be a positive one
and keep you happy most of the time.
If it is not, then it's a crime.
Don't let them get inside your head!

The people you speak to should help you grow
and not make you go soft and slow.
Don't let them get inside your head!

Do not let people drag you down,
and most of all, make you frown.
Don't let them get inside your head!

Devil's Dance!

Welcome to the Devil's dance,
he will put you in a trance
and look at you with a devilish glance.

The Devil is here to dance with you
and all your friends can come too,
believe me, because it's true!

Put together your best moves
because he wears his dancing hooves.
He'll swing you around so hold on tight
and by the end it will be a fright!

So welcome to the Devil's dance…
because you will not stand a chance!

Stress

Stress is a killer,
stress is a pain,
stress will cling to your heart
and squeeze on to your vein.
You have to relax,
you need to calm down,
you need to turn that frown upside down.
Stress will kill you if you give it half a chance…
So, don't invite it to the dance.

Chances

The chances are for me and you,
the chances are I haven't a clue!
The chance is for us to change,
the chances are to open our range.
The chance for change comes to us all,
the chances are that we might fall.
But that is life…I tell you so,
well don't just read this,
GIVE IT A GO.

Rhyme

Once upon a time,
there was a rhyme
about a man and a dog
and a chicken called Rod.
The chicken named Rod was such a sod,
the chicken named Rod thought he was a God.
But the man and the dog just smiled at Rod,
the cheeky little chicken sod!

Lockerbie

A night to remember,
21st of December.
Trying to get the decorations straight,
in the year of '88.
A Scottish town,
the folks didn't frown.
The night was young
and carols were being sung.
Then a bright light in the sky
that leaves us asking the question, 'WHY?'
Angels got their wings that night
and for family members it was a sorry fright.
They will always be in our thoughts, I know they can,
the angels on Flight 103, Pan Am.
The angels on the ground will stay to see
that nothing bad will happen again in Lockerbie.

It's Up to You

Mother and father or father and father,
mother and mother or auntie or gran.
They brought you into the world and helped you through time,
they cleaned your face when it was covered in grime.
They clothed you for schools
and taught you the rules,
and helped you when you didn't have a clue.
But now you're grown up and living your life
and getting yourself out of trouble and strife.
But never forget what they did for you –
from helping with homework or tying your shoe.
It's never too late to say thank you,
just close your eyes it's up to you.
Xx

Peach

Have you ever shared a peach with a chicken?
Well I have.
I took a bite and to my delight,
the chicken also wanted my half!
My hands were full of juice,
then the stone came loose;
she pecked it to the floor,
then she wanted no more.
She gave a little groan
and then a little moan.
Have you ever shared a peach with a chicken?
Well I have.

Blueberry Terry

Blueberry Terry lived in a chapel
and all day long ate slices of apple.
He had a chair that looked like a pear
and he didn't really give a care.
Blueberry Terry had a telly
and it was made out of strawberry jelly.
One day he started a rumour
about a long-legged satsuma;
she was a peach and was out of his reach,
she punched Blueberry Terry right in the belly
and kicked him in the plums!
There is a lesson here to teach…
Don't start rumours about a long-legged satsuma peach!

Magpie

The magpie in the sky was up to no good,
he clung to the gutter and pecked at the tiles.
The rooftops weren't safe for the sparrow race,
you should have seen the look on his face.

The magpie pecked and scraped with his claw
at everything the black and white saw!
He took to the sky looking for prey,
the sky was dark, gloomy and grey.

The magpie was up to no good that day.

Love

Don't let love suffocate you,
keep on going and never give in;
if you must, put the love letters in the bin.

The pain you're feeling will subside,
you will walk tall keeping your head up with pride.
If you need help, talk to your friend,
it seems hard now, but the pain will end.

Your heartstrings can be pulled,
your heart can be broken, so let your mind be awoken.
A broken vase can be fixed,
strength and courage are the mix.

Your Maker

What do you think you're on this planet for?
What do you think your maker saw?
You have your life,
you have to grow,
you have to plant the seeds you sow.
So, think about it in your head,
think of what your maker said.
Act on it before time runs out,
and if you struggle, give your maker a shout.
They will help you, but YOU
have to do the work too.

Lazy Susan

Lazy Susan, what are you doing to me?
Lazy Susan, why can't you see?
My heart is in a daze
and my life is in a phase.
You have me spinning around,
my feet can't touch the ground.
Our summer was great,
not being with you I hate.
Our lazy, hazy days
catching all the sun rays.
Our walks on the beach were such a treat,
but the sand was so hot on our bare feet.
I'll wait till next year to see you again, my dove –
my one, my only summer-time love.

The Mad Man

I'm not mad,
I'm not bad.
You can't lock me away,
I will have my say.
I sit in my cell,
this is hell.
I wish I could speak,
I wish I could tell.

The moonlit sky shines through the bars,
the aliens come and take me to Mars.
They will not listen; they think I'm crazy;
the drugs they give me make me hazy.
I feel so limp; I feel so lazy.

As I lie here, it's such a fright,
this straight jacket is way too tight.
The aliens will be back,
they'll be back for me;
I'll tell you this,
just wait and see.

This is Your Year

If you feel you're not at your best,
and you feel you need to rest;
if you're down but not yet out,
don't stay down and miss the count.

If you feel like you are trash,
come over here and graze our grass;
this grass is greener, this grass is lush.
This year make it yours, you're gonna have to push.

If you write, then write that bit more,
if your game is football, you must score,
if you play golf, then hit a four,
and if you're a boxer, don't hit the floor.

So set a higher line and make this year fine,
because this is your year,
your year to shine.
Your next chapter is going to be your headline.

Morning

The birds fly in the morning grey sky,
they swirl and twirl in between the trees so high.
A black and white cat sits on a beige rug
drinking some milk from a handmade mug.

My fingers tap as I play my records;
the tune gives a beat, it is a real treat.
The player's needle is a must,
spinning around whilst collecting the dust.

The old man outside walks his dog,
as I watch, rolling in, the mysterious fog.
It's been a strange morning, this morning it's been,
for open your eyes and see what can be seen.

Now lift your head up from out of your phone,
I tell you this once so please do not groan.
Life is too short for you to miss;
life is just grand. Life is just bliss.
Now jump on a bus or peddle your bike,
or go up a mountain for a good hike.

Just do something different to challenge your brain
and take your umbrella…it's starting to rain.

Down in the Dump

Smile, have you not?
Well, not for a while.
You are not happy,
you sad, sad old chappy.

Having a bad time, old boy?
Is life such a pain?
You feel like you're going insane?
It's not much fun being you,
but you have to stay true.
When your mind is like this
how you wish your life to be bliss.

But don't you worry, my son,
your time will come.
Work hard and it will be fun, and then
you'll soon be on a home run.

Farmer

The moon shines down on the valley below.
The farmer tends his field so slow.
The seamstress threads her cotton to sew,
and the runner wins the race by a toe.

We all need to do what we must do,
so I'll be me and you be you.
Don't be so harsh on others today;
go out and work, rest and play.

The Cat on the Windowsill

The cat sits on the windowsill staring at me like mad;
the cat sits on the windowsill and knows I'm very sad.
The cat sits on the windowsill and gives me a little smile;
the cat sits on the windowsill and knows I'll be all right in a
while.

The Kidney Stone

If a kidney stone could travel, where would it go?
Would it catch a flight to Moscow?
Would it drink alcohol and then be silly in Chile?
Would it fly to Japan, Taiwan and then Sudan?
Would it travel around Spain on a train?
Then would it fly to Rome, before heading home?

Sad

I'm really sad
because you think I'm bad,
and now that makes me really mad
because you just assume
that I've been rude,
instead of listening to my words,
you've just heard what you have heard,
and that's the end;
no second chance for me,
no chance to flee
the misery or the pain,
just the dishonour of disdain…
and that's a shame.

Pineapple Tree

Pineapple trees and orange groves,
blackberry pies and nobody dies.
We lose the seas to mushy peas,
the world is mad, the world is sad.
Am I bonkers? Chestnut conkers,
make coffee out of soil and lose palm oil.
Have I lost the plot dropping coins in the gaming slot?
I want to give love, release a dove,
then slap my face with a big rubber glove.

Budgie

The budgie swings and sways in her cage
looking like she's in a big rage.
Her head goes down
and her tail feathers pop up.
She spits her seeds on to the floor
and her plastic companion is a bore.
Her little mirror needs a clean
because her feathered face cannot be seen.
She sings so loud; she looks so proud.
She's only small but her spirit does glow…
that's our budgie. Our budgie, SNOW.

Dolly

You see the reflection in her eyes,
you see the reflection of the skies;
her face is smooth and silky to touch,
I love her, I love her so much.
Her little fingers are so cute,
her arms are small and she's not that tall.
Her dresses are old and not so bold,
her name is Polly, she is my porcelain dolly.

Close Your Eyes

Close your eyes and picture this…
a snake in the grass with a musical hiss.
Your mind is in a twist,
your thoughts are mist,
then your heart finds your brain and they have kissed.
You're at one
and your demons have gone.
You're reborn now, start afresh for heaven's sake…
and all because of the musical snake.

Today

Today is the day to start,
let all your past worries depart.
Let all your worries sink away,
let all your worries go astray.

Today is new and time to begin,
so put your worries in the bin.
You can turn this around and you will be sound,
just stop banging your head on the ground.

So grab them worries and that sin,
now throw them in the F#@KING bin!

This Day

This day has been so bad,
I've been so sad.
This day is so shitty,
I feel a lot of self-pity.
I can't get out of this mood,
I don't feel like having food.
The day is so crap,
I just want to nap.
I feel no excitement,
I feel no joy.
I'm not happy,
I'm a moody little chappy.
This day should end quick,
I feel so sick.
My head is taking the piss,
I can't be putting up with this.
Oh, all my sorrow,
hope I feel okay tomorrow.

Hard Night's Sleep

I couldn't get to sleep last night,
I was having to fight so hard;
I tossed and turned, up and down,
my face was such a frown.

The kitten was jumping on the bed,
then clawing at my fecking head;
I had to move on to the couch,
curl up and become a slouch.

The cats were scratching all night long;
the budgie started singing a song,
then in her cage
she became enraged.

Oh my God, the night was long,
then six o'clock I hear the gong.
I jumped off the couch and stood up straight,
my alarm clock was wrong…it was half past EIGHT!

Flowers

The flowers dropped in their bed,
the flowers dropped; they are dead.
Their petals did wilt on their head,
oh, my dear, the flowers are dead.
They were not blue, they are not red,
I gave them water, they were well-fed.
But to my surprise, the flowers are dead.

The Fallen Goose

Life has not been bad, but I cannot fly;
my wing is shot, I've had my lot.

I can't just leave you here,
you must get up and fly, my dear.

The human got me good,
my wing is blood;
you find the gaggle and take to the sky.

I cannot leave you and let you die.

It's not the end, my friend,
I will fly again, but not today;
now go, go I say.

We must take off, now get on my back,
we'll find the others and be back on track.

Quick you must go, the human comes with the hound,
but don't you worry, I'll be sound.

You will not be forgotten, I will always love you,
we will fly again that will be so true.

Crazy

You'll never believe this crazy fact,
so I'll tell you now and keep you on track.
Bananas are berries, but strawberries are not.
Cheetahs can't roar, but eagles do soar.
The clouds in the sky are heavy, that's true.
There are girls called Jack and men called Sue.
There are some jellyfish that never die,
and a group of monks that never lie.
Are these true, or are they not?
I can't remember, you know…I forgot!

Speckled Hen

The ginger-speckled hen lives in a dirty old den,
she pecks around all day and all night,
and keeps herself from human sight.
She feeds on corn and grit and dust
and cleaning her feathers is a must.
Jumping and hopping as she goes
and keeping a secret that nobody knows.
But I must warn you, don't be bad
and don't ever make the ginger-speckled hen mad,
because under her plumage the secret is kept,
one day she'll come out of her den
and then you will meet…SUPERHEN!

Time

Time moves on,
Christmas comes and goes.
What will happen next…
Nobody knows.

We do nothing with our lives,
but life moves on
and if we don't act,
soon we'll be gone.

When you're a child, a year is a lifetime,
the clock always ticks
and time passes quick,
but remember you don't have to be a spring chick.

You're as old as you feel
and age is but a number…
So, get out there
and become someone's thunder.

Fire

Fuel the fire; see what I see.
Will we grow? Let me see.
We can change, we can grow;
sow the seeds that we spill.
Leopards can change their spots;
you can change the lot.
Program your mind to be your best,
don't be lazy when put to the test.
Find that power and fuel your fire.

Be You

I'm proud of who I am;
I'm not black nor am I white –
and I'll tell you this,
I don't give a shite.

I'm not a woman and not a man –
and what you think, I don't give a damn.
If I was blind or deaf and dumb,
would you still be my chum?

If I was able-bodied or not at all –
I don't care, so sod you all.
You should be proud of who you are,
So, let them look and let them stare –
because in the end WE DON'T CARE.

Old Woman

The old woman on the train,
the man that looks in pain,
the child that takes the strain.
The world would be a better place
if only we had ONE human race.

The animals that suffer,
the killing fields get rougher,
the bullied people get tougher.
The world would be a better place
if only we had ONE human race.

The ice caps melt,
the forests dwelt,
we will have to live with the cards that are dealt.
The world would be a better place
if only we had ONE human race.

Religion at war – nobody wins,
and we all go to the same place for our sins.
The world would be a better place
if only we had ONE human race.

Feeding Time

Feeding time at dusk;
feeding time's a must.
The hens peck away at their seed;
the fat-man watching on with greed.
He sharpens his knives and greases his tray;
the chickens go in to lay.
The fat-man slips on a slither of fat and his knives fly in the
air;
the chickens watch on without a care.
The knives come down and slit his veins,
blood pours out like a leaking pen –
then in comes running the killer hen.
It drinks his blood with lust,
because feeding time is a must.
It's feeding time again.
It's dusk.

Plastic Tragic

The plastic bags, the plastic parts.
This is all plastic; this is all tragic.
It's in our oceans, it's in our seas;
it's on our land, it should be banned.
The micro-plastic we do not see,
it's in the fish that live in the sea;
it's then on your plate, then in your gut,
so in the future, do not tut.
Refuse to use plastic from this day on
and maybe the world might carry on.

Spinning Mind

My mind is spinning,
my patience is thinning;
I cannot think straight,
I have so much hate.

It's all in my mind,
but I must find
a way to stop this pain,
a way to break the chain,
or I'll go insane.

People can't see I'm not well,
there's nobody I can tell;
my God, this is hell.

Pain

We all suffer pain,
we all profit from gain,
we could all make money from the gravy train.
Life at times hits us hard,
life is bad if you choose the wrong card.
Choices in life are difficult to choose,
you might win,
you might lose.
Time passes by and we must try,
because in the end we all say goodbye.

Inclusion

Fifty years from now, what will be?
What will our eyes see?
Will there be me?
Will there be you?
Will your son or daughter be here too?

We can all do our little bit.
We can all do a little more;
we can compost our banana skins and apple cores.

Inclusion is the key;
the world will be here for you and me.
So include your family and friends,
so in fifty years the world won't end!

Lips of Love

Our lips did touch;
we loved so much.
Together we are,
together we stay
and our hearts will never be far away.
The smell of her skin,
the roughness of his chin;
our lips did meet in the darkness of the street.
Our love will stay strong,
our love will last long
just like our very own song.
We will always be in love,
down on Earth and above…
because we are so much in love.

What Are We Seeing?

Is it a green banana tree or is it a green sheep?
I close my eyes and see it in my sleep.
I cannot tell if it is a sheep of green,
but I do see it in a dream.
A green tree full of bananas;
I tell you this, I want no dramas.
A tree or a sheep, bananas or green;
what do you see now you have seen?

Write

I want to be light,
I want to write;
I want to be free
and I want to be me.
I want to be light like a kite in the sky,
I want to write with words that bring glee,
I want to be free like a fish in the sea,
but most of all, I want to be me.

Time Rhyme

It's time for a rhyme,
it's a rhyme about time…
We all have the same 24 hours in the day,
it's up to us to make it pay.
So don't waste the seconds
because we don't know what beckons.

Sin

They can crush you from within if you sin,
they can make your life hell if you don't tell,
they can drive you mad and make you sad.
You need to shout and let them out,
we are all flesh and bone, you're not alone.
Talk is good, I think you should.

Cambellwick Green

Cambellwick Green life is so mean,
but the streets are all clean in Cambellwick Green.
The cars do not run, they walk at one speed,
and over the fence is a steaming black steed.
You cannot hide, you will be seen on the clean streets of
Cambellwick Green.
The people are hell, but the music is swell.
There is one teen in Cambellwick Green;
he fights for his life with a swiss army knife.
The man walks the street with his flute in hand,
whilst all the children turn to sand.
It's an evil place that Cambellwick Green,
if you go, you can't be seen,
but the streets are very clean in Cambellwick Green.

Every Day

Every day counts, every day should;
I would enjoy every day if I could.
Life can be a chore, life can be a bore;
life could be irritating like a cold sore.
You awake in the morning to the sun, rain or the snow;
it could be the same, but just give it a go.

Hurry!

There's got to be something we can do about pollution,
there's got to be something;
there's got to be a solution.
The rubbish and filth that fills our bins;
the rubbish and filth, that's our sins.
We need to clean up our act,
we need to clean up today
…that's a FACT!

Normal

Normal, what is normal?
Am I normal?
Are you normal?
What is normal?
Is normal, normal?
What is the norm?
Is that normal?
I honestly believe I'm not normal!

Drunken Chickens

Intoxicated chickens on a Saturday night,
one fell over, one got into a fight.
Necking back whisky and ginger dry,
then on the dance floor they're not so shy!
Dancing all night with wobbly legs,
one spinning round with the other laying eggs.
Would these chickens be loved or hated…
simply because they're intoxicated?!

Pond Life

Pond life...with the green lily pad,
the butterflies and the frogs are never sad.
The flowers range from yellow to green,
and the underwater fishes are never seen.
You can sit there for days getting a suntan from the rays.
You'll never be happier; you can forget your troubles and strife,
because this is pond life.

Knives

When the knives come a falling,
when the broken hearts come a calling,
I'll be there for you.
When the knives come a falling,
stop your stalling,
I'll help you all the way through.
So, when the knives come a falling,
remember, start smiling...
because I'm always here for you.

I (Part II)

I love the wind,
the rain and the storms.
I love the sun,
the sand and the seas.
I love the trees,
the flowers and the bees.
I love to live,
I love to give,
I love to feel,
I love to be real.
But most of all,
I live to love.

Act Now!

Don't blame a generation,
don't blame creation.
Don't point the finger,
don't linger.
WORK HAS TO BE DONE.
Stop blaming the past.
We need to act fast;
we need to stick together.
WORK HAS TO BE DONE.
Generations stick together,
forget the past.
Break the mould and shatter that cast
because…TIME PASSES BY FAST!

Our World

The world we live in,
the world we love.
The Earth we ride on,
the Earth that spins;
we recycle our plastic,
we recycle our tins.
The oceans and seas are for our living,
the ocean and sea are our glee,
let's not dump, let us see…
Can we change the planet back to green and blue?
Do your bit, it's down to you.

The Mancunian Poet

Reasons why I'm me...
I'm unique, I am me;
my values are stronger than the roots on a tree.
I push myself and others to be their best;
I have tattoos on my chest.
I cheer you up when you're down,
and I can act just like a clown.
I like to sing in the rain
and sometimes I am a pain!
I'm not afraid for emotions to flow
and I'm always on the go.
I try to laugh every day,
but sometimes, well, hey!
Coffee is my favourite drink
and my favourite colour is pink;
if you're sad, I'd never let you sink.
I love my pets; I take them to the vets.
I love my home and I'd never roam.
I live in Manchester, that's where I want to be,
and this is the reason I am me.